Autographed Collectible Edition

EARTH'S BOUNTY
Healing Wisdom of Healthy Food

Gift Card

Date:

To:

From:

Message:

EARTH'S BOUNTY
HEALING WISDOM OF HEALTHY FOOD

Memoir, Self-Help, Nutrition

Earth's Bounty
Healing Wisdom of Healthy Food

Copyright ©2020 by Elaina Merlis

Website: www.EarthsBounty.life
Email: Elaina@earthsbounty.life

Paperback ISBN:
978-1-885872-42-5

E-Book ISBN:
978-1-885872-43-2

PCN:
2019916615

Published in the United States by
iPublishUGlobal
World's Only Full Service Publisher
Write, Dictate, Edit, Publish, Market, and Sales
Palm Beach, Florida

All rights reserved. No part of this publication may be reproduced, stored in a retrieval system, or transmitted in any form or by any means-electronic, mechanical, photocopy, recording, or any other-except for brief quotations in printed reviews, without the prior written permission of the author.

Cover and Book Design by Creative Genius
Sharon Esther Lampert

Photography by Elaina Merlis

Manufactured in the United States of America
First Edition

Earth's Bounty
Healing Wisdom of Healthy Food

iPublishUGlobal
LIVE FOREVER IN A BOOK
PALM BEACH, FLORIDA

HEALING WISDOM
OF HEALTHY FOOD

Dedication

I would like to express my gratitude to all those who supported me and my family through my illness/journey. This includes the Teaneck, New Jersey community, Greentree Acres family, and other family and friends who tirelessly worked to support and care for us during this trying time in our lives over seventeen years ago.

My husband, of blessed memory, who encouraged me throughout, would say, "Get out of bed, because you never know who you will meet today, how they may affect and help you, and how you may affect and help them." I hope that I am doing you proud, Mitchy!

Thank you to the creator who gives us all that we need to keep ourselves and the planet healthy. The rest is up to us!

FAIR USE NOTICE

In the US, section 107 of the Copyright Act of 1976, allows copyrighted material to be used for purposes such as teaching, education, research and a few other similar uses. We are making such material available in our efforts to advance understanding of issues of humanitarian significance, namely, nutrition.

Table of Contents

Introduction
1

Healing Wisdom of Healthy Food

Foraging
11

Gardening
23

Fermentation
33

Recipes
43

Did You Know?
83

Resources
87

Disclaimer

This book is not intended to provide and does not constitute medical or other professional advice. Please use this book as an inspirational resource.

Introduction
Open Heart

My name is Elaina Merlis. Thank you so much for allowing me to share my food and health journey with you.

If you would be so kind as to indulge me for a few moments, interlace your fingers behind your back, and lift your heart so that you can receive my message open-heartedly.

I am not a doctor or a nutritionist, or a professionally trained chef. That being said, I would like to tell you about myself. As a child, I grew up eating an animal-based diet, a lot of canned vegetables, as well as frozen foods.

My grandfather was a kosher butcher, and after the Wall Street Crash of 1929, my father's family relied heavily on the meat that wasn't sold that day for sustenance.

Therefore, it was only natural that I would grow up in a household that prioritized meat as a food staple as well.

Furthermore, as a teenager in summer camp, I was tasked with preparing chickens for cooking before the Sabbath. My thought process regarding what exactly we were eating shifted at that point.

When I returned home, I would not eat chicken in its form.

When I was a child, I was enamored with animals and plants. I was also interested in foraging, and learning what is edible in the natural world.

In the latter part of my childhood, we had a vegetable patch in our yard, and we went berry picking in the summer.

Fast forward a few decades, and I brought the love of nature and food into my preschool class. We grew carrots, watching the taproot and root hairs reaching to find nutrients. We viewed this process though old fish tanks and clear plastic soda bottles. We dried apple rings on string stretched across the classroom, and fermented our own pickles.

I taught the children that many of the things that we buy in the supermarket can be made and grown at home, and that the process of growing and preparing fosters a relationship between us and our food.

At 36, I became a pescetarian, thinking that fish did not have a complex nervous system, and that wild fish had a good quality of life before being caught. This does not mean that I maintained a healthy diet, because I was still consuming a lot of sugar and fried foods, as well as food containing white flour.

When I was 41, I was diagnosed with ovarian and endometrial cancer, and I had a radical hysterectomy, chemotherapy, and radiation. I couldn't complete my chemo because my platelets were being depressed by the medication that I was taking, so I opted to discontinue the chemo. In addition, the radiation depressed my white blood cell count, and they remain depressed to this very day. I get some relief by using imagery learned through the writings of Dr. Jerry Epstein, who believed in the mind-body connection. I would imagine my spleen with a clown's face laughing and spitting out healthy white blood cells.

Soon after healing from my "treatments", my oncologist told me that I was at a higher risk of having another cancer, and I asked him what I could do to prevent this, and he responded, "Just live!"

Then, interestingly enough, as I accompanied a friend who needed to have a breast core biopsy, and as luck may have it, I overheard a woman in the waiting room speaking about a Dr. Raymond Chang, MD, who offered some unusual but non-invasive immunity boosters.

I made an appointment with him, packed up documentation of my recent medical history, and went to see him. I believe that he has changed my life forever.

He explained to me how important certain foods were for maintaining a strong immune system and which foods I should omit. He told me to include wild mushrooms, such as maitake, shiitake, oyster mushrooms, lion's mane, among others.

He also underscored the importance of cruciferous vegetables, such as cauliflower, broccoli, kale, brussels sprouts, collard greens, red and green cabbage, and others.

Additionally, he discussed with me how green tea can help the body to fend off cancer, although the studies existing at the time did not recommend a specified amount of green tea intake. Dr. Chang recommended four to five cups per day.

Dr. Chang suggested keeping my sugars low and that included natural fruit sugar. Organic blackberries, blueberries, raspberries, and strawberries became my fruit mainstay. Aside from having low sugar, they are high in antioxidants, which boost your immune system. Dr. Chang presented me with the studies that provided the basis for his recommendations.

He suggested that I don't eat any "hormonal foods," as he called them, which include eggs and dairy products. He also advised me to stay away from foods that contain sugar or that could quickly become sugar, such as white bread, potatoes, and pasta. This was the beginning of a huge personal lifestyle change.

After practicing for a number of years, I realized that I had taken back my power, because I was feeling stronger. I had taken over a significant measure of control over my health, and I now no longer felt like a target.

Following the advice of Dr. Chang, I searched for foods that would not turn into sugar quickly. I learned that the trend of eating whole wheat bread as opposed to white bread was faulty, as whole wheat, which is finely milled, turns into sugar almost as quickly as white bread.

Next, I read the book Wheat Belly, by Dr. William Davis, and I learned why many people are suffering from celiac disease and gluten sensitivity. In a nutshell, wheat has been genetically altered, and it is difficult for the body to break it down.

In addition, I recently learned that wheat crops are heavily sprayed with glyphosate, a known carcinogen. This may also be the cause of intestinal discomfort from consuming wheat.

In line with the findings in the book, "Wheat Belly," Don Lewis, who runs Wild Hive Farm, located in New York State's Hudson Valley, produces ancient wheat. Mr. Lewis has told me that people who have had gluten problems have not had the same negative reaction when consuming his grain.

I then began to take classes at the Natural Gourmet Institute for Food and Health in New York City, and I realized how much I enjoy cooking and preparing beautiful, energizing real food that can support peoples' health.

One of the many things that I learned at the Institute was the art of natural fermentation. Interestingly, this process had been a part of my family's culture, as I remember seeing my grandmother, Bubby, with all of her jars and porcelain crocks on the kitchen counter.

Good gut health is one of the main benefits of fermentation, which counteracts the large amounts of antibiotics that most of us have ingested over the course of our lives. It takes time to build up healthy gut flora, so if we haven't been consuming foods with probiotics, it would be wise to begin to do so now. This can aid digestion, and help prevent acid reflux and digestive problems.

A Harvard Medical School article, "The Gut Brain Connection," asserts that gut and brain health are connected, so depression and anxiety may stem at least in part from poor gut health.

Other studies by reputable institutions on this topic have verified the connection between gut and brain health, and state that mood health can be supported by gut health.

These findings motivated me to start a small business producing fermented foods with a good friend of mine.

I ask that you pay attention to how you feel after eating and drinking fermented foods: Does it resonate with you? How does your body feel? Food should give you energy and make you feel alive. In my own experience, after I eat a heavily laden meal of simple-carbohydrate food (which is fiber-stripped), I feel tired, as opposed to a meal of slightly steamed or raw vegetables and fruits, which makes me feel more energetic.

Our environment is filled with toxins that we take in every day, and one of our greatest defenses is to eat nutritionally dense food that will strengthen our immune systems.

In recent years, I have turned to veganism, because I have dared to look at expose footage and documentaries on how animals are badly mistreated by the meat, poultry, dairy, and egg industries.

I also learned about the horrible effects that these industries have on the environment. It doesn't surprise me energetically that the abuse of creatures and the environment is linked to our own health.

A common problematic trend is that of "trendy" food items, as is witnessed in the case of kale. When the demand for kale peaked, mega farms seeking to maximize profit, mass produced kale, using pesticides and genetic engineering in the process. We see that in any mass production process, that when we lose our consciousness about how

Earth's Bounty: Healing Wisdom of Healthy Food

sentient beings and produce are raised, we cause disease.

For me and for those of you who are vegans and vegetarians, it is important that you monitor your intake of B-12. It can be supplied by eating raw fermented foods, and nutritional yeast. Most recently, I was reminded of that when I was reviewing my blood work with my doctor.

I encourage you to know your growers, because small farms, even those that are not organic are less likely to use heavy chemicals because they have more control over less space. In general, either organic or not, small farms are more likely to use sustainable methods that are better for our health and the planet. We have wonderful, trustworthy farmers right here in south Florida, such as Lox Farms, Gratitude Garden Farm, and Swank Farms to mention a few.

I also suggest that you grow some of your own food, which is not difficult. You can even regrow some foods by planting what you might otherwise discard, such as scallions, celery, lettuce, and others. It is important to connect with the miracle of how the earth provides you with sustenance and know that something bigger than you is providing support for your health.

Another way to get the most nutrient-rich food is by foraging. When a plant lives out in the wild, it fends off insects and disease by magnifyings its defenses, and those defenses are nutrient-rich for us. An example of this is purslane, which is rich in omega-3 fatty acids. I suggest that you connect with a local forager who can broaden your knowledge base.

Elaina Merlis

In my background, it is believed that one should not place herself in the public eye, because she may draw negative energy to herself. However, I know that I am giving my message to you with love, and that it will only be received with love, whether you accept what I have shared, or not.

In closing, please consider that eating consciously and kindly will raise the vibration of the planet and help you to live a joyful life.

HEALING WISDOM
OF HEALTHY FOOD

Elaina Merlis

HEALING WISDOM OF HEALTHY FOOD

FORAGING
Healing Wisdom of Healthy Food

Elaina Merlis

Elaina's Morning Forage
Coffee bean "cherries," Brazilian citrus,
star fruit, noni fruit, and rum bay leaves.

Earth's Bounty: Healing Wisdom of Healthy Food

Elaina's Foraged Coconuts
Young coconuts contain the most delicious, healthful, hydrating and full of electrolyte liquid.
Foraged from local South Florida coconut palms.
Can't get much fresher than that!

Elaina's Cashew Apple Forage
It may not look perfect but it's perfectly delicious

Earth's Bounty: Healing Wisdom of Healthy Food

Elaina's Forage

Nutritious sprouted coconut foraged this morning. It's a powerhouse of nutrition containing potassium, magnesium, calcium, phosphorus, manganese, omega-3 and omega-6 fatty acids, vitamin C, protein, iron, copper, vitamin A, fiber and healthy fat.

Elaina's Garden Brazilian Citrus Tree or Bakupari
The tree grows the most delicious little gems. They don't have much to eat on them but are packed with flavor.

Earth's Bounty: Healing Wisdom of Healthy Food

Elaina's Purslane
It's rich in omega 3 fatty acids.
It's a weed that packs a big healthy punch.

Elaina's Sea Grape Fruit

Known for aiding in digestive problems, proper function of the liver, are anti inflammatory and decrease cholesterol in the body. It contains a whole host of vitamins and minerals some of which are vitamins A, E, B2, folate, potassium, calcium, magnesium and iodine. They grow near the ocean or salt marshes and can handle high winds.

Earth's Bounty: Healing Wisdom of Healthy Food

Elaina's Lychee Season Has Begun!
Did you know that even though lychees contain mostly carbs and water, they also contain Epicatechin and Rutin, flavonoids that can help protect against heart disease and cancer. They're also high in vitamin C and contain a fair amount of copper and potassium.

Elaina's Noni Berry
Noni fruit has many health benefits but is malodorous when ripe. Best mixed with other fruit juices.

Earth's Bounty: Healing Wisdom of Healthy Food

Elaina's Monstera Fruit Forage

It looks like a large green pinecone. When the tile like scales fall off and show the white fruit with black thread like marks, it's ready to eat. It tastes like a mixture of banana and pineapple. It must be totally ripe, otherwise it can cause an itchy sensation in your mouth and on your lips. Per 100g: It contains 60mg of vitamin C, 23g of protein and 16g of calcium just to name a few of it's nutritional qualities.

Elaina Merlis

HEALING WISDOM OF HEALTHY FOOD

GARDENING
Healing Wisdom of Healthy Food

All these beautiful greens were picked fresh from my garden. What a gift from nature! Vibrant, beautiful food!

If you grow your own food and have more than you can eat, please donate some to the needy and help raise their vibration too!

Elaina's Herb Garden
Herbs and greens growing in my raised veggie bed,
begging to be made into a fresh salad.

Earth's Bounty: Healing Wisdom of Healthy Food

Elaina's Garden Fig
One beautiful fat green fig from my garden.
How I treasure Mother Nature!
Thank you G-d for nourishing us!

Elaina's Garden Figs

Freshly harvested figs from the garden with macadamia nut cheese, a drizzle of Bee Free honey made from apples, and red pepper flakes and a side of blackberriers.

Earth's Bounty: Healing Wisdom of Healthy Food

Elaina's Gifts from the Garden
Flowers and a small, sweet pineapple. The stack of cloth napkins are part of my effort to cut back on using paper goods.

Elaina's Garden Pineapple
The biggest pineapple I have ever grown from a second generation plant and it's still green! I expect that it's going to get larger before it starts ripening. I feel a grilled pineapple salsa coming on!

Earth's Bounty: Healing Wisdom of Healthy Food

Elaina's Fennel Flowers and Seeds
It's time to save seeds for the next growing season

ELAINA MERLIS

Elaina's Black Radish

The Black Radish

The black radish is sharp tasting with less water content that the red radish you're probably familiar with. Did you know that radish are part of the crucifer or brassica family? The black radish offers anti-cancer properties and help fight inflammation. Vegetables from the cruciferous family carry phytonutrients such as carbonyl (13C), a detox agent. There are research studies that show that they contain anti-estrogenic activity which may reduce the risk of contracting hormonal dependent cancers.

HEALING WISDOM OF HEALTHY FOOD

Fermentation
Healing Wisdom of Healthy Food

ELAINA MERLIS

Elaina's Coconut Jelly
Young coconut jelly keeps you satiated because it's a nutritiously dense food.

Earth's Bounty: Healing Wisdom of Healthy Food

Elaina's Fermented Foods for Healthy Gut Biome

Fermented foods are important for a healthy gut biome. This ferment is so easy to prepare.

Ingredients:
Coconut water and jelly from three young coconuts.

Instructions:
Step 1. Blend the coconut water and jelly until it's smooth.

Step 2. When the mixture reaches room temperature add the content of two probiotic capsules and mix with a wooden spoon.

Step 3. Pour the mixture into a sterilized glass jar and cover with cheesecloth.

Step 4. Secure the cheesecloth with a rubber band.

Step 5. Place out of direct sunlight and wait 24 to 48 hours.

Step 6. The timing is adjusted according to how sour you like your kefir.

Step 6. Use the kefir as the base for your favorite smoothie!

Hint: The most effective probiotics are the ones you find in the refrigerated section of your local health food store.

Elaina's Cashew Yogurt (Fermented) Parfait
Blackberries, ground flaxseed, walnuts, drizzle of maple syrup and mint.

Eliana's Cashew Yogurt Parfait

Homemade cashew yogurt with blackberries, ground flaxseed, walnuts, a drizzle of maple syrup and mint. If you'd like to try your hand at fermenting your own yogurt, here's the recipe.

Ingredients:
2 2/3 cups raw cashews soaked overnight
1 1/2 cups filtered water
4 tablespoons fresh lemon juice
1/2 teaspoon sea salt
3 probiotic capsules

Instructions:
Step 1. Drain cashews and place all the ingredients, except the contents of the probiotic capsules, into a blender and blend until smooth.

Step 2. Add the contents of the probiotic capsules and mix until well incorporated.

Step 3. Cover with cheesecloth and let it sit out in cool dark space for 24 hours.

Step 4. Refrigerate and enjoy.

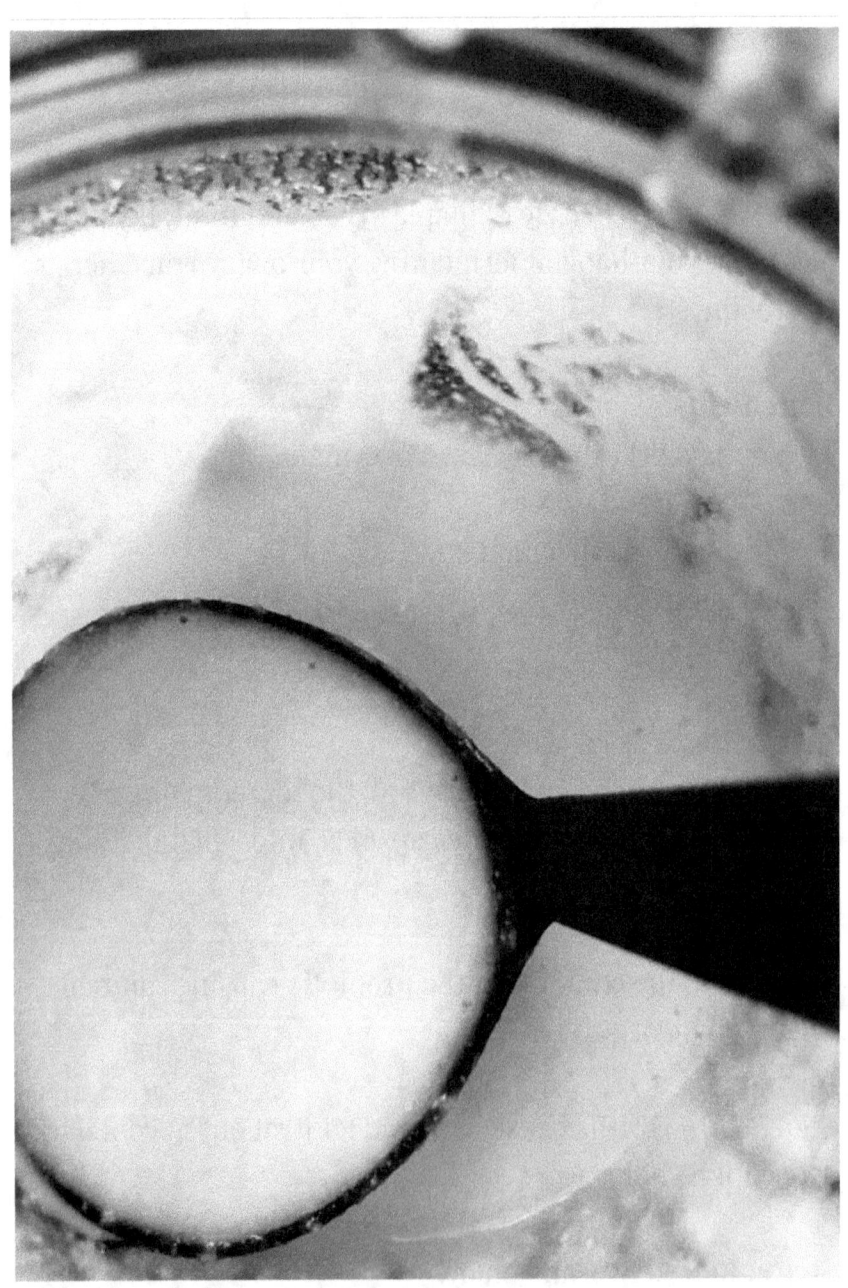

Elaina's Fermented Foods for Healthy Gut Biome

Elaina's Beet Kvass, Fermented Beet Drink

Elaina's Fermented Pickles
Making some raw fermented pickles. When I find small,
straight, Kirby cucumbers at the farmers markets,
I just have to put up a jar of pickles!
Take care of your stomach flora!

Earth's Bounty: Healing Wisdom of Healthy Food

Elaina's Fermented Lemons

Did you know that pasteurization kills good bacteria that we need for our gut health? Raw fermentation encourages the growth of beneficial bacteria or probiotics, and probiotics help with immune function and digestion.

Elaina Merlis

HEALING WISDOM OF HEALTHY FOOD

RECIPES
Healing Wisdom of Healthy Food

Elaina's Kiwi Cocktail
Tonight's cocktail of dandelion greens, fresh mint, Kiwi, homemade oat milk, maple syrup and crushed ice. Ahhhh!

Earth's Bounty: Healing Wisdom of Healthy Food

Elaina's Sprout Salad
Sunflower, pea, buckwheat, and radish sprouts with red onion and red pepper. They contain a large amount of living enzymes. Add dressing and feel your energy rise!

Elaina Merlis

Elaina's Garden Fig Salad

Nutritious Fig, carrot and romaine salad with apple chutney pomegranate vinaigrette and a light dusting of Brazil nut parmesan. These figs were harvested from my very own tree. It makes this salad all the more special!

Earth's Bounty: Healing Wisdom of Healthy Food

Elaina's Maitake Mushroom Saute'
Nutritious Maitake (known as hen of the woods) with roasted seminole squash, baby broccoli and onion with coconut aminos, garlic powder, ginger powder and red pepper flakes. Finish with cilantro leaves.

Elaina Merlis

Elaina's Gluten Free Oatmeal Dulse Crackers

Elaina's Gluten Free Oatmeal Dulse Crackers

Ingredients:
1/2 cup rolled oats
1/4 cup sunflower seeds
2 tablespoons coconut flour
1/2 teaspoon dulse granules with garlic
Pinch of sea salt
1 Tablespoon + 1 teaspoon melted coconut oil
1 Tablespoon + 1 teaspoon brown rice syrup or other liquid sweetener of your choice
1/2 tablespoon + 1/2 teaspoon filtered water
Seeds of your choice, sesame, poppy, caraway etc.

Directions:
Step 1. Grind oats and sunflower seeds in a food processor separately.
Step 2. Mix together and add coconut flour, dulse and salt.
Step 3. Pulse briefly.
Step 4. In a small bowl, whisk together coconut oil and rice syrup.
Step 5. Add wet ingredients to dry. Process until dough comes together, adding water as needed.
Step 6. Roll out dough between parchment sheets to about 1/8-1/4 inch thickness.
Step 7. Take off top sheet and score. Slide parchment with dough onto a baking sheet.
Step 8. Mix seeds and sprinkle generously onto dough, press down gently.

Elaina's Mild Smoked Spanish Paprika Vegetable Stew
Made with: tomato paste, carrots, sweet potatoes, parsnips, onion, green pepper, pinto beans, shredded Lion's Mane mushroom, vegetable broth, bay leaves, garlic powder, salt and black pepper.

Earth's Bounty: Healing Wisdom of Healthy Food

Elaina's Hot Lentils and Broth

Today's veggie was broccoli, but cauliflower, quartered brussel sprouts and asparagus work just as well. The lentils were made with vegetable broth, a few cloves of garlic, onion, bay leaves, salt and black pepper.

Elaina's Japanese Umeboshi Pickled Plum Dressing

This dressing will put kick into your salads as well as boost the nutritional value.

DID YOU KNOW?
According to Dr. Axe, umeboshi plums help cleanse the liver and fight cancer.

Ingredients:
1/2 cup avocado oil
1/4 cup rice vinegar
1 Tablespoon sesame seed
1 Tablespoon umeboshi plum minced
1 1/2 teaspoons lemon juice
1 teaspoon coconut sugar
1/2 teaspoon salt
Ground black pepper to taste

Instructions:
Place all of the above into blender and blend till smooth.

Earth's Bounty: Healing Wisdom of Healthy Food

Elaina's Japanese Umeboshi Pickled Plum Dressing

Elaina's Mushroom Salad
Warm grilled oyster mushroom and red onion salad with nutritional yeast dressing.

Elaina's Mushroom Salad

Warm grilled oyster mushroom and red onion salad with nutritional yeast dressing. Not only does nutritional yeast taste scrumptious but it contains vitamin B12.

Ingredients:
Nutritional Yeast Dressing
1/2 cup nutritional yeast
1/4 cup coconut aminos
1/3 cup Apple cider vinegar
1/4 cup water
2 cloves garlic
Pinch of cayenne pepper

Instructions:
Blend all of the above and then slowly pour in 1/3 cup extra virgin olive oil. Salt and pepper to taste.

Elaina's Creamy Cuke and Chickpea Salad
This dish is comprised of Persian cucumbers, chickpeas, red onion, fresh dill, unsweetened almond yogurt, rice vinegar, salt and black pepper.

Earth's Bounty: Healing Wisdom of Healthy Food

Elaina's Very Berry Smoothie
Dragon Fruit, blackberry, blueberry and cashew yogurt

Elaina's Seafood Salad

Shredded Lion's Mane Mushroom that I cooked in vegetable broth then drained and mixed with vegan organic mayo, diced celery, diced green pepper, fresh chopped dill, celery seed, fresh lemon juice, sea salt and black pepper.

Earth's Bounty: Healing Wisdom of Healthy Food

Elaina's Sprouted Tofu and Creamy Walnut Sauce
Spinach, oyster mushrooms and sprouted tofu in a creamy walnut sauce. The sauce is made with raw walnuts, olive oil, vegetable broth, garlic, fresh sage, salt and pepper.

ELAINA MERLIS

Elaina's Brown Jasmine Rice with Purple Kale and Walnut Sauce

Elaina's Brown Jasmine Rice with Purple Kale and Walnut Sauce

Walnut Sauce

Ingredients:
Raw walnuts
A few fresh sage leaves
A garlic clove or two (depending on how garlicky you like it)
1/2 a cup of vegetable broth
A splash of olive oil, salt and pepper to taste

Instructions:
Put it all in a blender and blend until creamy and smooth.

Organic Kale:
I tossed small pieces of raw kale into the finished hot brown rice and it was just enough heat to make it tender but not over cooked. This allows the kale to maintain its nutritive value.

DID YOU KNOW?
Please only use organic kale! Kale is heavily sprayed with a known carcinogen called glyphosate.

Elaina's Sprout Salad

Sprout salad made with pea and sunflower sprouts, cucumber, grape tomatoes, pine nuts, ground flaxseed (omega3), nutritional yeast (vitamin B12). Kalamata olives, pomegranate vinegar and avocado oil dressing gives this salad the Wow!

Earth's Bounty: Healing Wisdom of Healthy Food

Elaina's White Beans and Herbs
Soaked white beans and herbs, when cooked in vegetable broth or water, this becomes the most delicious soup, or topping for a rice dish, or puréed into a creamy sauce. So easy and versatile!

ELAINA MERLIS

Elaina's Cruciferous Powerhouse!

This simple dish of cauliflower, cucumber, parsley, red onion, mint, lemon juice, olive oil, sumac, cumin, sea salt and black pepper is a cruciferous powerhouse!

Earth's Bounty: Healing Wisdom of Healthy Food

Elaina's Sprout Salad with Grilled Artichoke Hearts
Grilled artichoke hearts, pea and sunflower sprouts,
raw pumpkin seeds, nutritional yeast, oregano, and
a red wine vinaigrette.

Elaina's Mushroom Cakes
Tarter Sauce, Red Cabbage Slaw and Wilted Spinach
Tarter sauce: homemade fermented pickles, capers, lemon juice, Kite Hill plain almond yogurt and vegan mayo.

Earth's Bounty: Healing Wisdom of Healthy Food

Elaina's Tempeh Broccoli
Coconut Aminos, Lime and Organic Sriracha

Elaina's King Oyster Mushroom Ceviche
Another way to include a low calorie, tasty,
cancer fighter in your diet.

Earth's Bounty: Healing Wisdom of Healthy Food

Elaina's Red Cabbage Salad
Served with roasted lions mane mushroom.
Two great cancer fighters in one delicious lunch!

Elaina Merlis

Elaina's Red Cabbage Vegetable Salad
Made with lemon juice and pea protein mayo in the works!
Love our cruciferous cancer fighters

Earth's Bounty: Healing Wisdom of Healthy Food

Elaina's Pumpkin Seed Collard Wraps
Pumpkin seed, cilantro and rice stuffed collard wraps with Thai dipping sauce made out of coconut aminos, sesame seed oil, lime juice, maple syrup, ginger, garlic, scallions and red pepper flakes.

Elaina's Baby Bok Choy

Baby Bok choy, shiitake mushrooms and sesame seeds with coconut aminos, sesame oil, ginger and garlic. Served with some rice for a quick, easy, tasty, and nutritious dinner.

Earth's Bounty: Healing Wisdom of Healthy Food

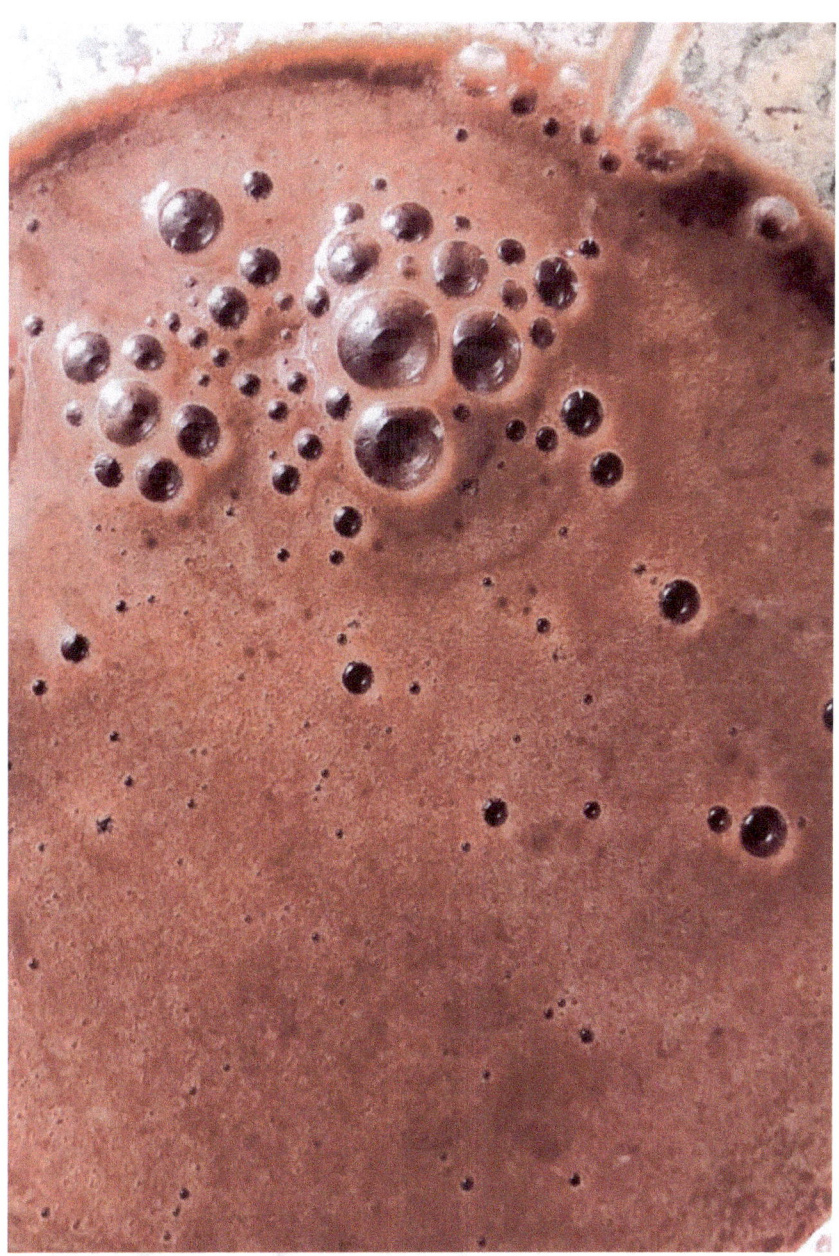

Elaina's Blackberry Tumeric Smoothie
Blackberry turmeric smoothie with young coconut water, cayenne, black pepper, and a touch of maple syrup. As delicious as it is healthy and beautiful! #anti-inflammatory

Elaina's Kale Salad
Kale, hempseed, dandelion greens, celery leaves, scallions, orange, shallot, apple cider vinegar, red pepper flakes, Himalayan salt and pepper.

Earth's Bounty: Healing Wisdom of Healthy Food

Elaina's Three Sprout Salad
Pea, broccoli, and mung bean with beautiful yellow tomatoes and hummus to top it off. A squeeze of lemon, a dash of olive oil and a pinch of salt and freshly ground pepper. Feel the energy rise!

Elaina Merlis

Elaina's Mushroom Soup Mix
The beginnings of a beautiful mushroom soup for Sunday's holiday boutique.

Earth's Bounty: Healing Wisdom of Healthy Food

Elaina's Vegan Mushroom Shawarma
Vegan mushroom Shawarma served with Persian green rice, lentils, broccoli, hummus and spicy green Schug.

Elaina's Lion Mane Mushroom Roast

These lions mane mushrooms were rubbed with olive oil and spices and roasted at 425° for approximately 35 minutes. So delicious and have tremendous health benefits.

Elaina's King Oyster Mushrooms
Browned in a little coconut oil and seasoned with pink Himalayan salt and freshly ground black pepper. Simply delicious!

Elaina's Mushroom and Dill Ragout
Made with Baby Bella, Maitake, Shiitake and King Oyster mushrooms. Season with nutmeg, dill, garlic, fresh black pepper and a splash of white wine or vegetable stock to deglaze the pan and bring flavor to this tasty nutritious meal! Serve over a baked potato, rice or quinoa.

Earth's Bounty: Healing Wisdom of Healthy Food

Elaina's Homemade Old Bay Seasoning

I didn't like all the additives that
I saw on the label of the supermarket
brands so I made my own.
The rum bay leaves that I foraged
for were perfect for this blend.

Elaina Merlis

HEALING WISDOM
OF HEALTHY FOOD

DID YOU KNOW
Healing Wisdom of Healthy Food

Elaina's Spice Rack

The Spice Rack

Did you know that spices as well as other foods are irradiated? It's done to kill bacteria, but it also destroys nutrients and reduces flavanols. Flavanols are phytonutrients that are important in supporting our immune systems. Some brands of spices are marked as non-irradiated and are more nutritionally in tact.

ELAINA MERLIS

HEALING WISDOM OF HEALTHY FOOD

Resources
Healing Wisdom of Healthy Food

Earth's Bounty: Healing Wisdom of Healthy Food

Recommended Books:

- Foraged Flavor by Tama Matsouka Wong with Eddy Leroux
- Food and Health by Annemarie Colbin
- Wild Fermentation by Sandor Ellix Katz
- The Kitchen Garden by Norma Coney
- Organic Gardening by Maria Rodale
- The Herb Garden by Malcom Hillier
- Wheat Belly by Dr. William Davis
- The Anti-Cancer Cocktail by Dr. Raymond Chang

Recommended Documentaries:

- Heal Yourself, Heal the World
- Food Matters
- Gerson Miracle
- Healing Cancer From Inside Out
- The Truth About Sugar
- Food, Inc.
- Farm to Fridge
- Cowspiracy
- Indigestible
- What The Health
- Forks Over Knives

www.ingramcontent.com/pod-product-compliance
Lightning Source LLC
Chambersburg PA
CBHW071022080526
44587CB00015B/2454